The Black man, the Father of Civilization, Proven by Biblical History

JAMES MORRIS WEBB, A. M.

Evangelist of the Church of God

(Acts 20-28, Biblical)

The
Black Man

The Father of Civilization

Proven by Biblical
History

AUTHOR:

James Morris Webb, A.M.

PREFACE.

I have many objects in presenting this book to the public.

First: I love my race regardless of the prejudice against her, the unenviable position she holds, and the things she is falsely said to be guilty of.

I demonstrate my love for her by launching this book before the public as somewhat of a defense against the prejudice of ancient, as well as modern historical writers and lecturers, who have misrepresented her, and took from her the good deeds and honors that are justly due her.

Secondly: I realize that my race has had defenders, and has some now, men of my race and men of other races. But I am simply presenting this book as an humble race defender, in connection with the body of race defenders, and if my theory in this book is accepted as one of the little fingers of this splendid body, I will feel that I have accomplished some results and thus portrayed the story of ''The Widow's Mite''— she gave all she had, and I contribute likewise.

Thirdly: To appreciate my argument, the reader had best have a Bible at his finger tips so as to examine my references and compare them with my statements, which I make wholly and solely upon the authorities found in the Bible, which in turn is the real and only authority on ancient history (again my authority is not inspired in the slightest degree with malice or hatred for the white race). My profession as a Minister of the Gospel of Jesus Christ would not permit me to defend in the name of justice, harboring malice and hatred or any ill feeling toward my white brethren. I am acting with that meek and humble spirit and with a gigantic pride in my race, which I hope, pleases God.

J. M. WEBB.

ABRAHAM LINCOLN   FREDERICK DOUGLAS
DR. BOOKER T. WASHINGTON

THREE OF THE GREATEST MEN
IN AMERICAN HISTORY

Frederick Douglas, the thunder-bolt, whose mighty peals of thunder awoke the sympathy of the Christian men and women of this country in behalf of his enslaved and suffering people.

Abraham Lincoln, the flash of lightning, who, like a streak of light from Heaven giving hope to the black people, struck the shackles from their hands and left them lying shattered at their feet.

Dr. Booker T. Washington, who is nobly directing a never-to-be-forgotten battle for that moral and industrial education, which Douglas and Lincoln made it possible for them to obtain.

INTRODUCTION

THE Bible gives the first and only true account of the origin of mankind. It is the only book containing an accurate record of the progress of man toward civilization, and it is the indispensable reference of all searchers after the real facts of the birth of humanity and its progress toward the civilization of today; beginning with his creation, it is the only authentic record of man; authentic because it is first hand, not a copy of something else or a scientific or literary review, but a dispassionate record of man's creation and progress, untrimmed, unshaped and unvarnished, to suit prejudice. It would not be a complete record if it did not show with the rest of them the origin of the black man and "Woe for all these pinnacle thieves"—it shows that he, the "black man" is the "father of civilization."

The black man has been misrepresented by prejudiced historians and lecturers. It has been and is now quoted that Ham, the father of the black man, was cursed by his father, Noah. Now, in regard to this incident let us take the Biblical record for it, and anyone not totally blind with prejudice will be convinced by reading in the Book of Genesis the 9th Chapter from the 20th to the 27th verse inclusive, that Noah did not, "for he could not curse" Ham, although he did in a fit of intoxication pronounce a curse on Canaan, the son of Ham. In passing, I might mention that Canaan was never inconvenienced by the curse of Noah, because he was the Father of seven prosperous nations, foremost among them were the Canaanites, Phoenicians and Sidonians. The Sidonians sprang from Sidon, who was the first son of Canaan, according to Genesis 10th Chapter 15th verse. These same Sidonians are the men "descended from black men" whom Solomon ordered Hiram of Tyre to engage to do the skilled hewing and designing of the timber work on Solomon's temple—Solomon declaring that these Sidonians, "black men" were the only men possessed with anywhere near sufficient skill to take charge of and successfully complete the artistic timber work on "His" Solomon's temple. First Kings 5th Chapter 6th verse speaks very plainly of this fact. Solomon knew the black race was a superior, not an inferior race. He married Pharoah's daughter—see 1st Kings, 3rd

Chapter 1st verse; 7th Chapter 8th verse, also the 9th Chapter and 16th verse. Solomon's wife might have been of as dark skin or even as black as he was, for history shows that Egypt had two full blooded Ethiopian Pharoahs just before and during the reign of Solomon, according to Herodotus, the names of these two Ethiopians were Sabaco or "Sebichos" and Sethos, so Solomon surely got an Ethiopian "Negro or black" woman for a wife. This naturally increased the proportion of Negro blood in the veins of the future King of the Jews. Viewing the progress of the immediate descendants of Ham we learn that a curse laid upon one by a mortal of that day was as foolish and ineffective as it is in this, the story about this curse, also the story of the black man who contended that a black skin and woolly hair is a disgrace, has, according to the Bible, no foundation. Speaking of black skin, the greatest brain work and wisdom ever given to this world was given by men of black skins, or at least in whose veins the greatest portion of blood was Ethiopian or Negro blood. As to this assertion and King Solomon, see "Songs of Solomon 1st Chapter 6th verse." Solomon's dark skin should cause no surprise, because his mother, Hittite, was also the widow of Uriah (see 2nd Samuels 12th Chapter 9th and 10th verses). The Hittites are the descendants of Heth and Heth was the second son of Canaan (see Genesis 10th Chapter 15th verse).

As to the woolly hair, Jesus, the Blessed Saviour of Mankind, will have His head covered with woolly hair when he comes to judge the world, (Daniel 7th Chapter 9th and 10th verses). Now, if Daniel's prophecy is true that when Christ left this earth he had woolly hair, he naturally will return with woolly hair, and the pictures of Him today are an erroneous conception of Him, by the artists. This grand old book the Bible, does not show that God ever turned a man black to disgrace him for his sins, or anything else, but this same Bible does show that God's power did turn a man white to disgrace him because of his sins, and said that his seed would be likewise forever. Facts are stubborn things and often very disagreeable, sometimes even sickening, and by reading carefully the 5th Chapter of the 2nd Kings, 25th, 26th and 27th verses, many of our highly civilized brethren "whose ancient ancestors disgraced them" will suffer an alarming fit of nausea. Among the many low cowardly things that

have been said and done against the Negro
during this Christian era, one poor be-
nighted individual published a "joke" in
book form, in which he claims that, the
Negro is a beast, the poor fellow tries to be
serious, and no doubt thinks he is offering
at least some proof of his assertion. The
poor fellow of course, receives some sympathy, and would no doubt receive as much
as any of the rest of his class, were it not
for the fact that he holds a Professorship
in one of our leading American Christian
Universities. Of course the disgust, if any,
is felt for those responsible for placing the
poor devil in such a position, and the real
and well placed sympathy is for the stu-
dent, who must suffer because of this fellow. The fact remains, however, that regardless of what has been said and done
against the Negro and of whatever might
be said or done against him in future, he is
the ONLY man who can trace himself back
through the ages to his origin, and find
monumental evidence of his unequaled
greatness, his prowess, the laurels and
great honors he won, the things he created
and perfected which have a direct influence
on our civilization of today.

The "black man" I boldly assert "was
the Father of civilization," born in the land

of Egypt, and the different branches of Science and Art were simply transmitted to other races, which, as the ages have rolled by have only been enlarged and to some extent improved upon. Even the modern American Negro has proven that he is original, for instance—as a Tonsorial Artist he has no superiors and no Negro was ever known to enter a "Barber College" to learn the trade. Negroes inherit the sweetest, most musical voices, and if you have not heard a Negro quartette or chorus after they have arranged the harmony of a piece they are to sing, you have not heard what is best and sweetest in vocal music. As instrumentalists "not forgetting the many others" I simply mention Blind Tom, and Blind Boone, the fame of these two men needs no comment. They only displayed that talent handed down to them through centuries by their black ancestors. As for the Negro being original, why the Negro has given great America the only claim she ever did or ever will have to a National music.

God honored the black man by allowing some of his Ethiopian blood to flow in the veins of His only Son Jesus Christ, and I unhesitatingly assert that Jesus would in

America be classed a NEGRO. I make this assertion only on the authority of the Bible, according to which Jesus was born out of the tribe of Judah. Judah had only five children and they were males, (1st Chron. 2nd ch. and 4th v.), three by his first wife and two by his second wife (1st Chron. 2nd ch. 3rd and 4th vs.), and both of his wives were descendants of Canaan, a black man who was the son of Ham (Genesis 10th ch. 6th v.). Tamar, Judah's second wife, bore him two of these sons whose names were Phares and Zarah (1st Chron. 2nd ch. and 4th v.), these two names appear in the genealogy of Jesus Christ in the Book of Matthew (1st Chapter 3rd verse), so it is no trouble to see that Judah of whom Christ was to come, started out by presenting to the world children of Canaanite women who were Hamite descendants. Now, Virgin Mary, of whom Christ was born was beyond all doubt a woman out of the tribe of Judah, and every Bible reference proclaims that Jesus was to spring from this tribe of Judah (Genesis 49-10, Heb. 7-14, Rev. 5-5th). Our beloved St. Paul tells us in (Romans 1-3) that Jesus was of the seed of David according to the flesh. David is the 10th man named from Judah in the genealogy of Jesus Christ (Matthew 1st

Chapter, 3rd, 4th, 5th and 6th verses). Added to this David's great, great grandfather "Booz" was born of the woman Rahab, who was a direct descendant of Ham (Matthew 1st Chapter 5th verse). This also shows that David, one of God's greatest soldiers, was one who most successfully led his people and one who had Negro blood in his veins. Bible history is full of honors for the Black Man, Jethro the Ethiopian or Negro father-in-law of Moses, who was the author who first employed that, which is today, our judicial system, considerably twisted and revised to meet the changing conditions of civilization (Exodus 18th Chapter). This chapter tells of Jethro's visit to Moses, and how he gave Moses the foundation of what is today our system of graded courts for pronouncing judgments. Again Moses "The Hebrew Emancipator" was named by a black woman "Pharoah's daughter"—she said she called him Moses because she drew him out of the water (Exodus 2-10) and besides black men educated Moses. At any rate he received what education he had in the schools of the black people of Egypt (Acts 7th 22nd), so there is nothing remarkable in the fact that Dr. Booker T. Washington, W. E. B. DuBois, W. S. Scarborough and many other Negro or black men occupy places among the foremost and most eminent educators of the world, and why should they not? They are descended from fathers who ruled Egypt centuries ago and with their great wisdom layed the foundation of learning.

BISHOP H. M. TURNER, D.D., L.L.D.

The Most Fearless Defender the Afro-Americans Have

BISHOP H. M. TURNER, D.D., L.L.D.,

Bishop H. M. Turner, born at Newbury, South Carolina, February 1st, 1833, is the senior Bishop of the A. M. E. Church. He has been Bishop for thirty-one years, and is quoted as the walking encyclopedia of Methodism, and for this cause the last general conference that convened at Norfolk, Va., on May, 1908, voted unanimously for the good Bishop to be the historian of the African-Methodist Episcopal Church. It is to be remembered that Bishop Turner was the first colored man to be a commissioned officer in the United States Army, which appointment he received from President Lincoln. The Bishop was twice a member of the Georgia Legislature, and also the first of his church to be elected Bishop to Africa.

THE BLACK MAN

FIRST CHAPTER.

"THAT time changes all things" is a saying so old and so true as to admit of no argument. It is exemplified in so many different ways as to require no comment, and yet when we hear the phrase used glibly and thoughtlessly, every day, it is but natural to wonder if the one who uses it realizes what he is saying, or rather, if he knows what those few commonplace words mean, when used to form that sentence.

It is a foregone conclusion that he does not. He never stopped, "he, of this enlightened age, I mean," long enough to examine even a little of the abundance of indisputable proof that the saying "Time changes all things" applies to things and conditions, seldom if ever present, to his own narrow mind, and far away and beyond even his meaner and low prejudiced influence. If he did, his retrospective mood, would, before carrying him back to the very beginning, suffer something of a shock, and his attitude would change. Instead of delighting in history, modern, medieval and

ancient, his attitude would change so notice-
ably that an observer would imagine that
his only interest was in tearing down and
falsifying facts, and concealing records that
he could not falsify. When we hear or read
the sayings of some of our "misnamed"
great men, but in reality disgustingly conspicuous public figures, we are fully justi-
fied in making the charge of falsifying and
concealing such facts as they are not really
ignorant of. One of these conspicuous public characters delights in making the assertion that the Hamite Ethiopian or Negro
never amounted to anything, or possessed
anything, never occupied an eminence, save
to which the Semitic or white man had
dragged or driven him up to. If ignorance
alone was responsible for this glaring false-
hood, a great deal of sympathy would go
out to those who make the statement as well
as those who believe it to be true because of
their ignorance. As harsh as it may seem
sympathy would be wasted for a great deal
of the self asserted enlightenment of today
is but egotism. Much of the so-called wisdom is self praise for successfully concealing, or at least surrounding historical facts
with such mystery as to place the descendants of Shem upon an eminence which is
not justly his and makes him in his own

opinion appear much larger than what he
really is. And yet with all the egotism,
some knowledge of the true origin of mankind exists, and it is this knowledge that
causes the fasifying and hiding as much
as possible the true historical records, especially of the black man. It cannot be said
that the learned historical writers, the great
Divines, Theological students and lecturers
of today are ignorant of the history of
Ham, the son of Noah, and his descendants,
such as Nimrod, the founder of the great
ancient city of Babylon, and also Menes
the first King of Egypt and the founder of
the great ancient city of Memphis.

Ridpath says that the traditions of an-
tiquity points to Memphis and Babylon as
the fountains of human wisdom. If those
above-named are ignorant of the history of
the last-named, they are doing the world a
great injustice in assuming the position of
teacher and leader. If they are familiar
with the history of the races and the deeds
of men, they will no doubt have for them
and their kind good and sufficient reasons
for making false and misleading statements
as to some historical records, and totally
forgetting or demeaning others.

An early Queen of Egypt was a descendant of the Ethiopian or Negro race.

This is conceded by some of the modern writers; some of them going so far as to say that her skin was very black, and a few of them acknowledge that it was this black queen who placed the first fleet of war ships on the river Nile. They have no doubt traced this woman back to where they are satisfied that she was descended in a direct lineal line from Zipporah, the black and Ethiopian wife of Moses. We read very little of these two women, because modern writers seek to obscure them, and our ministers of the gospel never preach or lecture on that part of the Bible in which they are mentioned. WHY? Because, if they do they must give credit to black people. In this connection, I do not speak of Biblical history only. Were it not for the fact that the dimensions of this book would be extended far beyond what was intended, I could begin even with Hannibal, the Carthagenian General, and record the accomplishments of black men without the intervening of any long periods of time, down to the time of Alexander Dumas, Toussant L'Overture, and Alexander Sergievitch Pouskin, Russo-African poet. I could do more, I could come into the borders of this Republic and beginning with Crispus Octikus, or Alexander Hamilton—record the accomplishments of these same black descendants of Ham, down to this day. This modern record would contain many references to both the war of Independence and the war of the Rebellion. It would also mention a great many black men who can never forget El Caney and San Juan Hill. Besides the heroes of war, modern history is replete with the names of black men famous in peace for their accomplishments in science and letters of art. Space will not permit me to dwell upon these men and their accomplishments and the towering obstacles in spite of which they succeeded. I could not fail, however, to mention Frederick Douglas who was one of the greatest statesmen America ever had, even though he was born a slave. Dr. Booker T. Washington was also born a slave, and is one of the greatest educators the world has ever known. As to the many other great things black men have done and are doing, I cannot fail to mention the north pole, for, if human beings have stood on the spot claimed as the north pole, the black man was preceded by no one. I speak of Mr. Matt Henson, the Negro, who, if indeed, the pole ever was reached, was one of the first of the only two "to date" to reach it.

PROF. W. S. SCARBOROUGH

Prof. W. S. Scarborough is head of the Classical Department of Wilberforce University of Ohio, and Vice-President of the same institution. He, too, is a great writer in defense of the Afro-American race. Here are some of his remarks in his master-piece, "Race Integrity": (See next page.)

"The truth is that the term 'Caucasian' has little or no meaning as it is now used. The word itself is a conventional term given at the first by Blumenbach to designate what he considered the highest type of the human family, shown by a skull from Mount Caucasus. When we attempt to trace those who would claim the name as an expression of their superiority we find the type has disappeared. There is no pure specimen now in existence. And if we ask what is 'white' we can only say, 'that it is a term used to designate the absence of color'—that is all, and no sign whatever of 'race integrity.' We have already indicated that science and investigation point to the fact that primitive man was not white. It is no new theory, but it has seemed convenient for the Saxon to let it rest as much as possible in discrete oblivion. Bishop H. M. Turner of the African Methodist Episcopal church has often promulgated it in his own inimitable way, and Moncure D. Conway has also declared that the white people of the world today are only a reflex leprosy and that the natural color is brown or black."

SECOND CHAPTER.

HIS FIRST HOME

God but faintly revealed the puzzle of civilization to Noah and his three sons, Shem, Ham and Japhet (Genesis 9th Chapter 1st seven verses), and it became their duty to start to work on the first moves of the puzzle, as well as to create nations. He, who would begin from the first, moves and works the matter out to perfection.

Ham, the father of the black man, located in Africa. Africa was his homestead, so to speak. David, the Psalmist, credited Ham with this territory in the 105th Psalm 23rd and 27th verses, and also in the 106th Psalm 22nd verse. Now, if this is not true, and we reject it on the ground of not being sufficient proof of the black man's first and original home, we can on quite as good ground reject any and every other part of the Bible, for what I here state is no wild imagination, but FACTS taken from the Bible.

Cush, Mizriam, Phut and Canaan were the first sons of Ham (Genesis 10th Chapter, 6th verse), and these four sons including Nimrod, the grandson of Ham, were the first to start work on the problem of civilization; in a word they were the pioneers and the very pillars of civilized governments.

Cush located in South Egypt on the River Nile. He became the father of the Ethiopians as well as the father of the Cushites through Nimrod who located on the Southern part of the Euphrates River. It is to be remembered that Nimrod is the founder of the Babylonian kingdom (Genesis 10th Chapter, 10th verse.) Mizriam located on the upper part of the River Nile, and he became the father of the Egyptians. Phut located in the Northern part of Africa. Canaan located in the land known as the old Palestine country, which is modern Turkey. Canaan became the father of the Canaanites (Genesis 10th Chapter, 15th, 16th, 17th, 18th and 19th verses). According to the Bible the above is the exact location of the first sons of Ham, and the question which naturally follows is, "Was civilization born in their land and given birth by Ham's first offspring?" It is conceded by John Clark Ridpath and a few other writers on ancient history that the Egyptians were the fathers of civilization, according to the chronology of Manetho, an Egyptian priest. Egypt was founded in the year B. C. 3892, and Menes was the first mortal King. The all important question now arises, "Were the Egyptians descendants of black men, or were they descendants of white men? Were they descendants of Ham or Shem?" It is well known that students claim to be divided in their opinion as to the original stock from which the ancient Egyptians came. Ridpath, among others, says they were neither Semitic nor Negro, but concludes his remarks on the origin of the Egyptians by saying that the ancient Egyptians were considered a branch of that part of the Cushite family, which settled in Asia. Probably the little matter of the Cushites being the grand-children of Ham slipped Ridpath's mind, else his statements would not have been so conflicting, because he just says that they were not Negroes, but ends his argument by saying that they were a branch of the Cushite family of Asia.

It requires no laborious research to establish the facts that Cush was the father of all Cushite nations. He was also the first son of Ham (Genesis 10th Chapter, 6th verse). Now then, if the Ethiopians and all other Cushite nations who sprang from this first son of Ham were not Negroes, will

some of our historians omit the word
"probably," so much used by them, and say
what they were. It is fair to assume that
with their boasted intelligence and superior
brain power, by this time they would have
been able to search out and connect at least
some of the many facts, and plain, indisputable records in the Bible which leaves
no room for doubt or "probably."

We learn from the Bible that Ham is the
father of the African family; the Ethiopian
is the darkest or blackest tribe of the Ham-
ites. Cush was the founder or father of this
tribe. Moses selected his wife from this
black or Ethiopian tribe (Numbers 12th
Chapter, 1st verse). It must be plain to
any one who will read the parts referred
to in the Bible, that Ridpath's contention
that the Egyptians sprang from the Cushites was the wrong avenue to escape
the blood of the Negro, or their relation to the black man's family. I believe,
however, that Ridpath wrote in good
faith for the majority of the historical writers claim that the Egyptians descended
from a white race, notwithstanding they
admit that the Old Testament gives the
truest, the most complete and reliable record on the origin of the Egyptians of any
other book, so it is not unnatural to believe

that their opinions are influenced by racial prejudice.

Now it is true that the Bible contains the only authentic, and certainly the most ancient record of not only the Egyptians, but of all mankind, and I CAN and will PROVE by it that the Egyptian—Hamite—sprang from Mizriam.

According to the Biblical Gazette, the word "Egypt" is derived from the word Mizriam, and this word "Mizriam" was the name of one of the first sons of Ham (Genesis 10th Chapter, 6th verse). By the word "Egypt" being coined from the word "Mizriam," it strengthens my contention that the Egyptian was descended from the black man. I will now dig down further into the rich earth of proof for more enlightenment out of the Book of Truth. By viewing the ancient Bible map of Africa and Asia, which map can be found in the back of the New Testament, one can readily pick out the spots upon which Shem, Ham and Japheth first located. You will notice that Mizriam, the second son of Ham, and the accredited father of the Egyptians located on the very spot, so to speak, where the great City of Memphis was built by Menes, the first King of Egypt. Again you will notice that all

the names within African borders are
names of the sons of Ham, Shem and his
offspring, located in Asia. Perhaps a bet-
ter way to locate Ham, Shem and Japheth
and their first offspring is first to read the
10th and 11th Chapters of Genesis, then
locate their names on the map, and it will
be seen that not a Shemite, or white man,
originally located in Africa. All of the
white men located in Asia, and according to
the Bible white men never began to travel
in Africa until Abraham's time, B. C. 1921.
The Egyptians lived in a high state of civilization near 2,000 years before Abraham's
first visit to Egypt, and the appearance of
white people was a circus and a curiosity to
the black people. Abraham realized this
fact and commanded his wife to represent
herself as his sister, because as he said,
"she was fair to look upon," white (Genesis 12th Chapter, 11th, 12th and 13th verses). This would indicate that the Egyptians were not white, and I will say without
fear of my assertion being disproven, that
until after the time of Abraham, the Egyptians were a simon pure black race. Shortly
after Abraham's visit, the Shemitic or
white travellers began to pour into Egypt
to such an extent that the Egyptians began
inter-marrying with them, and of course,

this inter-marrying had its effect of contaminating the pure Negro blood, and this inter-marrying was the cause of the black man, or full blooded Egyptian losing the power of control in the Kingdom. In other words—this is the loop through which the Shepherd or white or Shemitic kings slipped through and took possession of the Egyptian kingdom.

DR. W. E. BURGHARDT DUBOIS

Dr. W. E. Burghardt DuBois is the most scholarly speaker and writer of the Afro-American race. He is the author of the book "Souls of Black Folk," which is a marvellous book. On the following page are some of the phrases from his famous address to the Social Study Clubs of Chicago University,

February 13th, 1907, on Education and Civilization:

"The doing of the world's work is a great duty and a great privilege. It is a thing not to be aimed at but to be aimed beyond. Just so soon as a nation or a country can put its foot upon this satisfaction of the lower wants and step upward to the greater aspirations of human brotherhood and the broader ideals of civilization, just so soon the real building of civilization begins. It seems to me, therefore, that the students of Chicago University and they that teach them, ought especially, on every occasion to impress this broader aspect of the race problem. That instead of putting it in its narrower, nastier channel, instead of stooping to listen to men, who themselves represent what is lowest and least in our national organization, that you should strive in every way to realize yourselves and to show others that this great broad question of humanity is not a question of petty crime, not a question of so many bales of cotton, not a question even of mere industrial development, but is a question of human aspiration, and that if here in America, on the very fore front of present advance, it is possible to murder the aspiration of 10,000,000 of men, then America is not yet civilized.''

THIRD CHAPTER.

HIS RULE IN EGYPT

Dr. Leonhard Schmitz, Ph. D., LL. D., F. R., S. E., says in his work on ancient Egyptian history, that these Hyksos or Shepherd Kings were Semite people. "White," of course, and they comprised the 15th, 16th and 17th dynasties, which covered 511 years. Now, during this period, Jacob and his twelve sons and their families moved from Canaan to Egypt, and other Semite or whites from Asia did likewise, because the white man had begun to rule Egypt. At the 18th Dynasty, however, fortune turned against the white rulers of Egypt, and the black men or the Negroes regained possession of their country, and banished the whites from their land, except the Jews, whom they held as slaves. They reorganized the Kingdom with their own blood, "the blood of the Negro." Aahmas was the first King after the whites were driven out, and his wife was Nefruari, the Ethiopian Princess, greatly celebrated for her dusky charms, her wealth and her accomplishments. The beginning of this reorganization of a period is recorded in the 1st Chapter of the Book of Exodus, which shows that at the beginning of the slavery of the Jews, God told Abraham that his people would be held in bondage in Egypt for 400 years (Genesis 15th Chapter, 13th verse). Those 400 years marked the period of Egypt's most rapid and substantial progress, as Dr. Schmitz says in writing on ancient Egyptian history, those years were the most brilliant in Egypt's record, and the period at which her art reached its highest point. It is but reasonable to suppose this to have been so, for the Shepherd, or "white Kings" had destroyed all of the former brilliancy of Egypt, and did not because they could not do anything to replace or imitate its grandeur or beauty. The black people when they regained possession of their Kingdom and again began to rule, made slaves of the Jews and compelled them to do all the heavy, dirty, unskilled labor, such as carrying bricks and mortar and working in the field (Exodus 1st Chapter, 13th and 14th verses). While the Egyptians turned their attention to science and art and reorganizing and drilling their army, so as to be able to protect their country against all nations. As Dr. Schmitz says, the Eastern boundaries of Egypt were well protected by strong fortresses. This is but natural, because on the East, the Semitic or white races reigned, and no doubt they were unfriendly to the Egyptians, or "black" people, because they had expelled the Shepherd or "white" Kings from their land. Now, when the Egyptians had attained "in that Age" to the highest degree of intelligence and wisdom, and were possessed of the greatest human power, God deemed it wise to make His own Infinite wisdom and power felt over that of human wisdom and power, by using Moses as an instrument to knock at the door of the Egyptian government and ask for the release of the enslaved Jews. Moses did not appear in Egypt by any human authority, or power, but by the authority and the power of God, for it would have been useless for not only Moses, but for any nation or number of nations to approach Egypt with hostile intentions, without God, because Egypt with her wisdom and power had the world at her mercy. There it required God with His immeasurable wisdom and power to overcome the wisdom and power of these black Egyptians. The evidence of God's power was displayed to the "Pharoah Meneptah," who is generally conceded to be the "Pharoah of the Exodus," by His, "God's" instruments, Moses and Aaron who were to appear before the Pharoah and cast down their rods which turned to serpents (Exodus 7th Chapter, 10th verse). When they had cast down their rods before Pharoah, and they turned to serpents, Pharoah called the wise men, or magicians of Egypt with their enchantments, and they cast down their rods which also became serpents (Exodus 7th Chapter, 11th and 12th verses). This was the performing of two miracles, one by God's power, and one by human power. This vieing with God, though only for an instance of time is what no white man has had the power to do since his creation. But, however, God, in order to demonstrate His supreme power, caused the serpents transformed from the rods of Moses and Aaron to swallow the serpents transformed from the rods of Pharoah's or Egypt's wise men (Exodus 7-12). This rod and serpent incident was the beginning of a series of plague miracles (read the 7th, 8th, 9th and 10th Chapters of Exodus), which wrecked the Egyptians' or black man's kingdom, and also destroyed that great power which he had over all other nations and released the Jews from slavery.

The black man's power, as the first power among the nations had now begun to decay, and as the black race began to die, as a power among nations, the white race began to rise to where it had never been before, but this was 2,500 years after the black man had worked out all the problems of civilization.

In reading Revelation, 13th Chapter, 11th verse, of St. John, the Divine, I am very much impressed by the description of one of his revelations which God unfolded to him, and which he describes as follows:

"I behold another beast coming up out of the earth and he had two horns, like lamb's, and he spake as a dragon." Now, to my mind, the foregoing vision of St. John the Divine, was this very country, the United States of America, revealed to him ages ago before this country was discovered and named, the two horns I interpret to be the two great political parties, that have done so much to corrupt this Government and misrule its people from their infancy to the present day. Again, the American Government spake like a dragon when it permitted slavery to exist, especially when its Constitution says "That ALL MEN WERE BORN FREE AND EQUAL."

Now, concerning the creating and inthralling of nations, their rise and fall, that is the will and the work of God. (75th Psalms, 6th and 7th verses.) (Jeremiah, 27th and 5th verses.) (Daniel, 2nd Chapter, 21st verse.) (Daniel, 4th Chapter, 17th verse.)

So, since it is true that the black man is the father of civilization, it is just as true that the white man is now at the helm, and the big "I AM" of the civilized world. But the fact remains that he took his civilization and his position after the black man had created it, and passed from the stage of action, just as the white man must do at God's own appointed time, to make room for some other race, probably the yellow race, Chinese or Japanese. David, the Psalmist, said: "Egypt was the land of the black man—Ham not Shem, the white man," and he further said that the Tabernacles which were the houses and dwellings from the lowest to the King's palaces were Ham's, and not Shem's, the white man— (Psalms, 106th Chapter, 22nd verse; 105th Chapter, 23rd to 27th verse; 78th Chapter, 51st verse).

It is easy to understand why the Negro or black man is not identified with his Egyptian brother; that reason is seldom honestly and earnestly sought for. The reason is—that the historians, with a very few exceptions, write from a prejudiced standpoint, together with the fact that they do not give credit to the Old Testament, if indeed, they study it at all, especially that part of it which is the most ancient, and beyond all shadow of a doubt the first and only TRUE account of the origin of mankind it is easy to understand.

It is impossible for God to forget that the black man and his land (Egypt) was the cradle of rescue that rocked and nursed the Son of God in his first two years of life, when Herod's decree to destroy all children under two years of age was issued. It was known that the decree was issued for the express and only purpose of destroying the infant Christ, but God chose Egypt, the black man's land, as a haven of rest and safety during the life of the displeased and would-be infant murderer, Herod. (Matt., 2nd Chapter.)

This might be the origin of that old, old saying, "Blood is thicker than water," for Jesus in going into Egypt, went among black women and men, who were the founders of the tribe from which he sprang.

When God in His infinite wisdom, His great love, justice and mercy, and at His own appointed time, summons mankind to take his rightful place in the wavering human line to be rewarded for that smallest of virtues, in proportion as he for the greatest of virtues, will say to the black man, who will be found heading the line, "Well done, thou good and faithful black servant, thou, My instrument, the Father of Civilization."

THE END.

COMMENTS ON LECTURE TOURS
OF THE WRITER.

To Whom It May Concern:

"I beg to say, after hearing Elder Webb on the subject, that the blood of the Negro coursed through the veins of Jesus and Solomon. I am frank to say I have seldom, if ever, enjoyed such an intellectual treat. The position he assumed as the subject of his lecture touching the Hametic blood and race is difficult and requires a practical knowledge of Biblical and historical lore. But I am pleased to say that he not only shows himself an expert, but the master of the situation, and I commend him to the ministry and churches of our race of every denomination.   Truly,

"BISHOP H. M. TURNER."

COMMENT FROM ONE OF THE LEADING PAPERS OF THE WRITER'S HOME.

"The evidence submitted by Elder Webb tending to prove that the Saviour of mankind was a black man seems to be sufficient to put those who oppose the proposition upon their proof. Now that the chain of evidence presented by Mr. Webb appears so complete, it is strange that none of the delvers in the Biblical records have not advanced the sensational proposition before. Not only was Christ a Negro, but it seems that Solomon, who has been held up through all of the ages as the personification of wisdom, had Ethiopian blood in his veins also.—*Seattle Daily Times.*

HENRY O. TANNER

The World-Famous Afro-American Artist

Henry O. Tanner is the world famous Afro-American artist. He is the oldest son of Bishop Tanner of the A. M. E. Church. He was born in Pittsburg, Penn., but was trained in the public schools of Philadelphia, to which place his parents moved soon after his birth. His first steps in his life work were taken in the art schools of Philadelphia from which training he went to Paris where his genius developed and flowered in the studies of Benjamin Constant and Julien. In 1895 his "Sabot Maker," was shown in the salon exhibit and received friendly treatment from the French critics. Frenchmen, as a rule, are not too favorably inclined to the works of foreigners and their appreciation of Tanner is truly significant of the real value of his work—a merit which puts it beyond the limitations of race and country. In 1896 he exhibited "Daniel in the Lion's Den," the first of a line of religious works with which his fame has been since connected. This picture received Honorable mention from the French Jury and was bought by the Pennsylvania Academy.

Mr. Tanner's picture, "The Two Disciples at the Tomb," was purchased by the Chicago Art Institute for $1,600.

In Memory of

Paul Lawrence Dunbar

Famous
African-American
Poet

THE COLORED SOLDIERS

(From Dunbar's "Lyrics of Lowly Life.")

If the muse were mine to tempt it
  And my feeble voice were strong,
If my tongue were trained to measures,
  I would sing a stirring song.
I would sing a song heroic
  Of those noble sons of Ham,
Of the gallant colored soldiers
  Who fought for Uncle Sam!
In the early days you scorned them,
  And with many a flip and flout
Said "These battles are the white man's,
  And the whites will fight them out."
Up the hills you fought and faltered,
  In the vales you strove and bled,
While your ears still heard the thunder
  Of the foes' advancing tread.

Then distress fell on the nation,
  And the flag was drooping low;
Should the dust pollute your banner?
  No! the nation shouted, No!
So when War, in savage triumph,
  Spread abroad his funeral pall—
Then you called the colored soldiers,
  And they answered to your call.

And like hounds unleashed and eager
   For the life blood of the prey,
Sprung they forth and bore them bravely
   In the thickest of the fray,
And where'er the fight was hottest,
   Where the bullets fastest fell,
There they pressed unblanched and fearless
   At the very mouth of hell.

Below are written some of the comments on his poetry and prose:

Dr. Adams, editor of "The Advance," says: "Dunbar was a genius bound in ebony."

Former President Theodore Roosevelt said: "I was a great admirer of his poetry and his prose."

"

P. KA ISAKA SEME
A NATIVE BORN AFRICAN

P. Ka Isaka Seme, who delivered such a wonderful oration on the subject, "THE REGENERATION OF AFRICA," which oration is reproduced from the Colored American Magazine of New York (June, 1906). This oration substantiates me in my article wherein I claim that the black man was the FATHER OF CIVILIZATION.

The Regeneration of Africa

Curtis Medals Oration, First Prize, April 5, 1906, Columbia University

I HAVE chosen to speak to you on this occasion upon "The Regeneration of Africa." I am an African, and I set my pride in my race over against a hostile public opinion. Men have tried to compare races on the basis of some equality. In all the works of nature, equality, if by it we mean identity, is an impossible dream! Search the universe! You will find no two units alike. The scientists tell us there are no two cells, no two atoms, identical. Nature has bestowed upon each a peculiar individuality, an exclusive patent—from the great giants of the forest to the tenderest blade. Catch in your hand, if you please, the gentle flakes of snow. Each is a perfect gem, a new creation; it shines in its own glory—a work of art different from all of its aerial companions. Man, the crowning achievement of nature, defies analysis. He is a mystery through all ages and for all time. The races of mankind are composed of free and unique individuals. An attempt to compare them on the basis of equality can never be finally satisfactory. Each is self. My thesis stands on this truth; time has proved it. In all races, genius is like a spark, which, concealed in the bosom of a

flint, bursts forth at the summoning stroke.
It may arise anywhere and in any race.

I would ask you not to compare Africa to
Europe or to any other continent. I make
this request not from any fear that such
comparison might bring humiliation upon
Africa. The reason I have stated,—a common standard is impossible! Come with
me to the ancient capital of Egypt, Thebes,
the city of one hundred gates. The grandeur of its venerable ruins and the gigantic
proportions of its architecture reduced to
insignificance the boasted monuments of
other nations. The pyramids of Egypt are
structures to which the world presents nothing comparable. The mighty monuments
seem to look with disdain on every other
work of human art and to vie with nature
herself. All the glory of Egypt belongs to
Africa and her people. These monuments
are the indestructible memorials of their
great and original genius. It is not through
Egypt alone that Africa claims such un-
rivalled historic achievements. I could have
spoken of the pyraimds of Ethiopia, which,
though inferior in size to those of Egypt,
far surpass them in architectural beauty;
their sepulchres which evince the highest
purity of taste, and of many prehistoric
ruins in other parts of Africa. In such

ruins Africa is like the golden sun, that, having sunk beneath the western horizon, still plays upon the world which he sustained and enlightened in his career.

Justly the world now demands—
"Whither is fled the visionary gleam,
Where is it now, the glory and the dream?"

Oh, for that historian who, with the open pen of truth, will bring to Africa's claim the strength of written proof. He will tell of a race whose onward tide was often swelled with tears, but in whose heart bondage has not quenched the fire of former years. He will write that in these later days when Earth's noble ones are named, she has a roll of honor too, of whom she is not ashamed. The giant is awakening! From the four corners of the earth Africa's sons, who have been proved through fire and sword, are marching to the future's golden door bearing the records of deeds of valor done.

Mr. Calhoun, I believe, was the most philosophical of all the slave-holders. He said once that if he could find a black man who could understand the Greek syntax, he would then consider their race human, and his attitude toward enslaving them would therefore change. What might have been the sensation kindled by the Greek syntax

in the mind of the famous Southerner, I
have so far been unable to discover; but oh,
I envy the moment that was lost! And woe
to the tongues that refused to tell the truth!
If any such were among the now living, I
could show him among black men of pure
African blood those who could repeat the
Koran from memory, skilled in Latin,
Greek and Hebrew,—Arabic and Chaldais
—men great in wisdom and profound knowledge—one professor of philosophy in a
celebrated German university; one corre-
sponding member of the French Academy
of Sciences, who regularly transmitted to
that society meteorological observations,
and hydrographical journals and papers on
botany and geology; another whom many
ages call ''The Wise,'' whose authority Ma-
homet himself frequently appealed to in the
Koran in support of his own opinion—men
of wealth and active benevolence, those
whose distinguished talents and reputation
have made them famous in the cabinet and
in the field, officers of artillery in the great
armies of Europe, generals and lieutenant
generals in the armies of Peter the Great
in Russia and Napoleon in France, presi-
dents of free republics, kings of independ-
ent nations which have burst their way to
liberty by their own vigor. There are many

other Africans who have shown marks of genius and high character sufficient to redeem their race from the charges which I am now considering.

Ladies and gentlemen, the day of great exploring expeditions in Africa is over! Man knows his home now in a sense never known before. Many great and holy men have evinced a passion for the day you are now witnessing—their prophetic vision shot through many unborn centuries to this very hour. "Men shall run to and fro," said Daniel, "and knowledge shall increase upon the earth." Oh, how true! See the triumph of human genius today! Science has searched out the deep things of nature, surprised the secrets of the most distant stars, disentombed the memorials of everlasting hills, taught the lightning to speak, the vapors to toil and the winds to worship—spanned the sweeping rivers, tunneled the longest mountain range—made the world a vast whispering gallery, and has brought foreign nations into one civilized family. This all-powerful contact says even to the most backward race, you cannot remain where you are, you cannot fall back you must advance! A great century has come upon us. No race possessing the inherent capacity to survive can resist and remain unaffected by this influence of contact and intercourse, the backward with the advanced. This influence constitutes the very essence of efficient progress and of civilization.

From these heights of the twentieth century I again ask you to cast your eyes south of the Desert of Sahara. If you could go with me to the oppressed Congos and ask, what does it mean, that now, for liberty, they fight like men and die like martyrs; if you would go with me to Bechuanaland, face their council of Headmen and ask what motives caused them recently to decree so emphatically that alcoholic drinks shall not enter their country—visit their king, Khama, ask for what cause he leaves the gold and ivory palace of his ancestors, its mountain strongholds and all its august ceremony, to wander daily from village to village through all his kingdom, without a guard or any decoration of his rank—a preacher of industry and education, and an apostle of the new order of things; if you would ask Menelik what means this that Abyssinia is now looking across the ocean—oh, if you could read the letters that come to us from Zululand—you, too, would be convinced that the elevation of the African race is evidently a part of the new order of things that belong to this new and powerful period.

The African already recognizes his anomalous position and desires a change. The brighter day is rising upon Africa. Already I seem to see her chains dissolved, her desert plains red with harvest, her Ayssinia and her Zululand the seats of science and religion, reflecting the glory of the rising sun from the spires of their churches and universities. Her Congo and her Gambia whitened with commerce, her crowded cities sending forth the hum of business, and all her sons employed in advancing the victories of peace—greater and more abiding than the spoils of war.

Yes, the regeneration of Africa belongs to this new and powerful period! By this term regeneration I wish to be understood to mean the entrance into a new life, embracing the diverse phases of a higher, complex existence. The basic factor which assures their regeneration resides in the awakened race-consciousness. This gives them a clear perception of their elemental needs and of their undeveloped powers. It therefore must lead them to the attainment of that higher and advanced standard of life.

The African people, although not a
strictly homogeneous race, possess a common fundamental sentiment which is every-
where manifest, crystalizing itself into one
common controlling idea. Conflicts and
strife are rapidly disappearing before the
fusing force of this enlightened perception
of the true intertribal relation, which relation should subsist among a people with a
common destiny. Agencies of a social, eco-
nomic and religious advance tell of a new
spirit which, acting as a leavening fer-
ment, shall raise the anxious and aspiring
mass to the level of their ancient glory.
The ancestral greatness, the unimpaired
genius, and the recuperative power of the
race, its irrepressibility, which assures its
permanence, constitute the African's greatest source of inspiration. He has refused
to camp forever on the borders of the industrial world; having learned that knowledge is power, he is educating his children.
You find them in Edinburgh, in Cambridge,
and in the great schools of Germany. These
return to their country like arrows, to drive
darkness from the land. I hold that this
industrial and educational initiative, and
his untiring devotion to these activities
must be regarded as positive evidences of
this process of his regeneration.

The regeneration of Africa means that a new and unique civilization is soon to be added to the world. The African is not a proletarian in the world of science and art. He has precious creations of his own, of ivory, of copper and of gold, fine, plaited willow-ware and weapons of superior workmanship. Civilization resembles an organic being in its development—it is born, it perishes, and it can propogate itself. More particularly, it resembles a plant, it takes root in the teeming earth, and when the seeds fall in other soils new varieties sprout up. The most essential departure of this new civilization is that it shall be thoroughly spiritual and humanistic—indeed a regeneration moral and eternal!

O AFRICA!

Like some great century plant that shall
     bloom
In ages hence, we watch thee; in our dream
See in thy swamps the Prospero of our
     stream;
Thy doors unlocked, where knowledge in
     her tomb
Hath lain innumerable years in gloom.
Then shalt thou, waking with that morning
     gleam
Shine as thy sister lands with equal beam.